Play It!

LEVEL 1

A Superfast Way to Learn Awesome Songs
on Your Piano or Keyboard

CHRISTMAS SONGS

By Jennifer Kemmeter and Antimo Marrone

G
GRAPHIC ARTS
BOOKS®

Library of Congress Control Number: 2019951376

ISBN: 9781513262512 (paperback) | 9781513262529 (hardbound) | 9781513262536 (e-book)

Proudly distributed by Ingram Publisher Services.

Published by Graphic Arts Books
an imprint of West Margin Press

WEST
MARGIN
PRESS

WestMarginPress.com

WEST MARGIN PRESS
Publishing Director: Jennifer Newens
Marketing Manager: Angela Zbornik
Editor: Olivia Ngai
Design & Production: Rachel Lopez Metzger

Contents

Hi Kids! My Name is Zooey. I'm going to teach you how to play music. Using my awesome system, you don't need to know anything fancy or technical— all you need is to know your colors, be able to follow a tune, and maybe even sing along. It's easy! Once you learn my cool, color-coded system, you'll be able to play a bunch of songs you probably already recognize, just by pressing the colors on the keyboard. Let's play!

Good Piano Posture
also known as The Pro's Pose!

It may not seem important at first, but when you
sit down to play, the way you sit on the bench or chair
plays a part in how good your music sounds.
Follow this diagram to look and sound like a pro:

1 Let your upper arms hang loose and relaxed from your shoulder.

2 Keep your back straight and lean forward slightly.

3 You want your elbows slightly higher than the keyboard to
get the best sound from the keys (you may need to adjust the
seat height or sit on a book to get things just right).

4 Sit on the front half of the bench or chair so that your
weight is positioned forward toward the keyboard.

5 Position yourself so that your knees are slightly underneath
the keyboard.

6 Keep your feet flat on the floor. If they don't touch, put some
books or a step underneath them.

7 Use rounded hands to strike the keys—hold your wrists above
the keyboard and arch your fingers down toward the keys.

That's it! Now you look like a rock star!

How to Use This Book

Now that you look cool at the keyboard, you're just five steps away from playing your first song! Here's how:

1 **Cut out the color-coded labels** on page 65 or 67. Be sure to set aside the red "Middle C" label, because this one is special. The letters on the labels represent the musical notes on the keyboard. So, red labels represent C notes in music; yellow labels represent E notes; blue labels represent G notes; etcetera.

> **TIP:** *To make the labels last longer, ask your parent or teacher to laminate the sheet of labels before cutting them.*

2 **Attach the "Middle C" label to the keyboard.** It's the one nearest the center of the keyboard that's shaped like an "L". You can use tape or removable blue putty to secure the label.

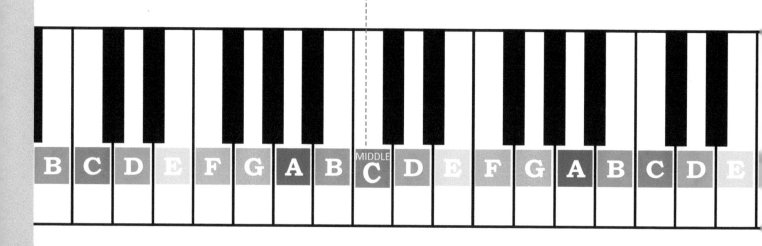

Middle C is the C key nearest the center of the keyboard.

B C D E F G A B C D E F G A B C D E

3 Once you have attached the Middle C, **follow the diagram** on the top of the pages for the song you want to play to attach the rest of the color-coded labels.

> *TIP: Put any loose labels into a covered container and tuck them into a drawer or your piano bench for storage.*

The Itsy Bitsy Spider

4 Again referring to the diagram, **place your hands in the correct position** for playing the song. Then, shift your attention to the song and begin to play, pressing the keys with the colors and using the correct finger as shown.

Twinkle, Twinkle Little Star

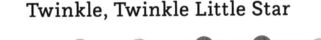

Twin - kle, twin - kle, lit - tle star,

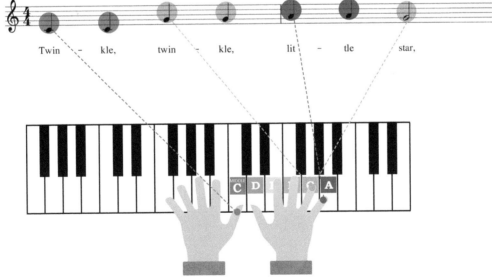

5 **Have fun!** Once you get the hang of it, you'll be able to play a ton of new songs. Look for me throughout the book—I'll be giving you extra tips and tricks so you'll become even more of a rock star as you go.

Let's Get Started!

Before you dive in and play your first song, I want to tell you about a few things you're going to see in the pages that follow.

First, you'll notice that each song is shown on a series of five horizontal lines. This set of lines is called a **staff**. You don't need to worry about this yet—your focus will be on the colors—but the music notes get placed on the staff and represent specific keys on the piano.

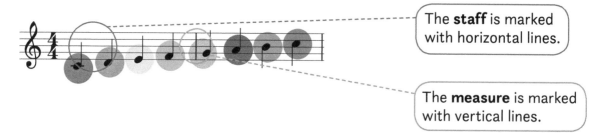

The **staff** is marked with horizontal lines.

The **measure** is marked with vertical lines.

Next, the staff is divided into individual sections, each separated by a vertical line. Each section between the vertical lines is called a **measure**. These measures help divide the song into smaller bits that make it easier to learn how to play.

There's also something called the **time signature**. The time signature tells you how to count the music.

 The top number tells you how many beats are in each measure. (Ignore the bottom number for now.)

For example, if you see: there are 4 beats in the measure

there are 3 beats in the measure

 there are 2 beats in the measure

Time to Warm Up!

Professional rock stars always warm up before their gigs.
Here's a cool way for you to warm up too—the scale.

1 Follow the diagram below to attach the color-coded labels to
the keyboard.

2 Starting with your left pinkie and ending with your right pinkie,
play each colored key one at a time.

3 Do the same thing again, only backwards: start with your right
pinkie and play each note until you reach your left pinkie.

4 Repeat steps 2 and 3 a few times until your fingers feel nice and
loose. Do this every time you sit down at the keyboard.

Now, let's try some exercises.

Exercise 1

Good to know: If you see a note that looks like

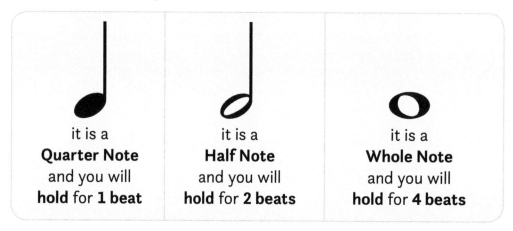

| it is a **Quarter Note** and you will **hold** for **1 beat** | it is a **Half Note** and you will **hold** for **2 beats** | it is a **Whole Note** and you will **hold** for **4 beats** |

Now you try: Clap out the **rhythm** and **sing.**

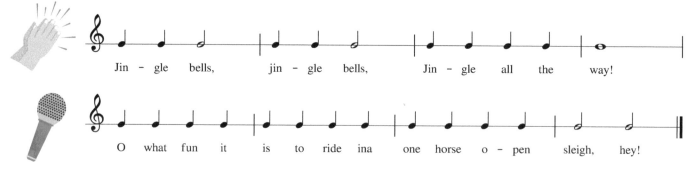

Jin – gle bells, jin – gle bells, Jin – gle all the way!

O what fun it is to ride ina one horse o – pen sleigh, hey!

Start to play: Using your right hand, practice the notes you will play.

RESTING PLAYING

Got it? Good. Let's try playing the first two songs.

Jingle Bells

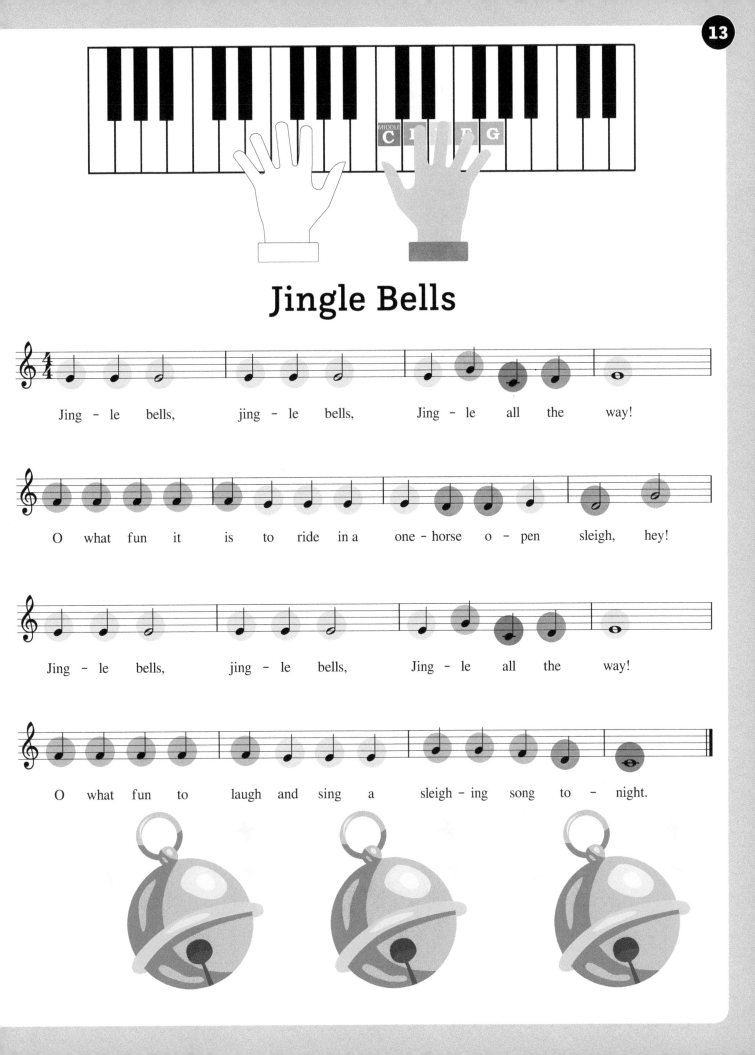

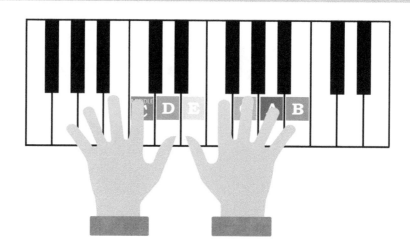

Jolly Old Saint Nicholas

Jol – ly old Saint | Ni – cho – las | lean your ear this way. | Don't you tell a
When the clock is | strik – ing twelve | When I'm fast a – sleep | Down the chim – ney

sin – gle soul | what I'm going to | say. | Christ – mas eve is | com – ing soon,
broad and black | with your pack you'll | creep | All the stock – ings | you will find

now you dear old | man, | Whis – per what you'll | bring to me | tell me if you | can!
hang – ing in a | row | Mine will be the | short – est one | You'll be sure to | know.

Repeat
1 time

Exercise 2

Remember: The notes are placed on the staff in a specific way.

The notes in the **spaces** spell

F A C E

Say it 5 times: *"If it's in a space, it's part of FACE."*

The notes in the **lines**

E G B D F

can be remembered in a sentence:

"Every Good Boy Deserves Fudge."

Say it 5 times: *"Every Good Boy Deserves Fudge."*

Exercise 3

Remember: If you see a note that looks like

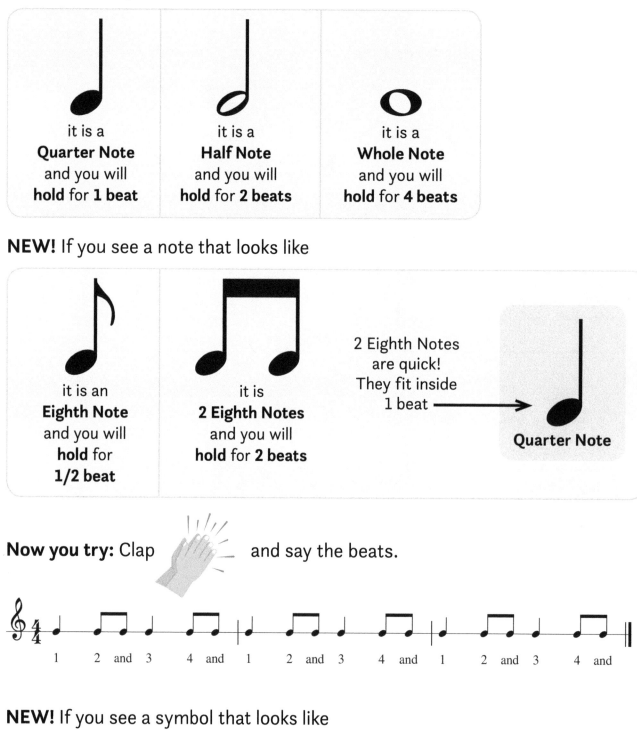

it is a
Quarter Note
and you will
hold for **1 beat**

it is a
Half Note
and you will
hold for **2 beats**

it is a
Whole Note
and you will
hold for **4 beats**

NEW! If you see a note that looks like

it is an
Eighth Note
and you will
hold for
1/2 beat

it is
2 Eighth Notes
and you will
hold for **2 beats**

2 Eighth Notes
are quick!
They fit inside
1 beat ⟶

Quarter Note

Now you try: Clap and say the beats.

1   2   and   3   4   and   1   2   and   3   4   and   1   2   and   3   4   and

NEW! If you see a symbol that looks like

it is an
Eighth Note Rest
and you will
rest for **1/2 beat**

it is a
Quarter Note Rest
and you will
rest for **1 beat**

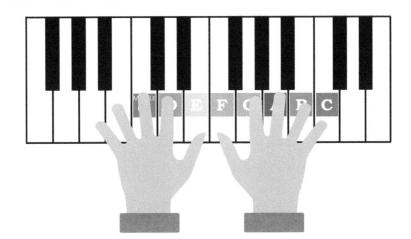

Christmas is Coming

Chris - mas is com – ing, the goose is get-ting fat. Please put a pen-ny in the

old man's hat. If you have not got a pen-ny, a ha' pen-ny will do, If you

have - n't got a ha' - pen - ny, well – God bless you.

Exercise 4

Good to know: If you see a note that looks like

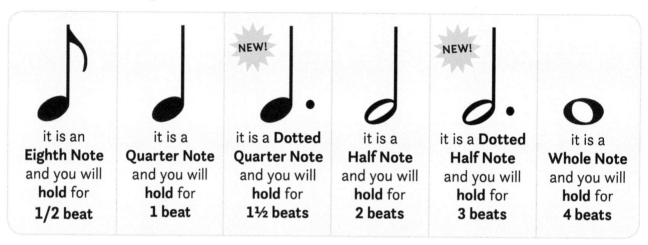

it is an **Eighth Note** and you will **hold** for **1/2 beat**	it is a **Quarter Note** and you will **hold** for **1 beat**	NEW! it is a **Dotted Quarter Note** and you will **hold** for **1½ beats**	it is a **Half Note** and you will **hold** for **2 beats**	NEW! it is a **Dotted Half Note** and you will **hold** for **3 beats**	it is a **Whole Note** and you will **hold** for **4 beats**

Now you try: Clap and say the beats.

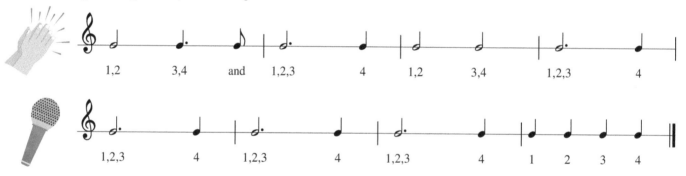

Try one more time: Clap and sing.

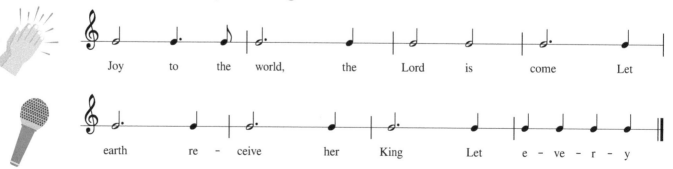

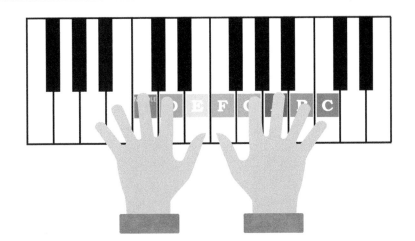

Joy to the World

REMEMBER: The dot means add half the value of the note.

Count: 1, 2 | 3, 4 | and | 1, 2, 3 | 4

Joy to the world, the Lord is come Let earth re -
Joy to the world, the Sa - vior reigns! Let men their

ceive her King Let e - ve - r - y he - a - rt pre - pa - re Hi - m -
songs em - ploy While fie - lds and flo - od - s and rocks and hills and

room An - d Heav - en and Na - tu - re sing An - d Hea - ven and Na - ture
pla - i - ns Re - peat the sound - i - ng joy Re - peat the sound - i - ng

sing An - d Hea - ven and Hea - v - en and Na - ture sing.
joy Re - pea - t Re - pe - a - t the sound - ing joy.

Repeat
1 time

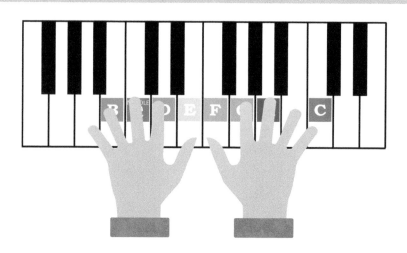

Here We Come A-Caroling

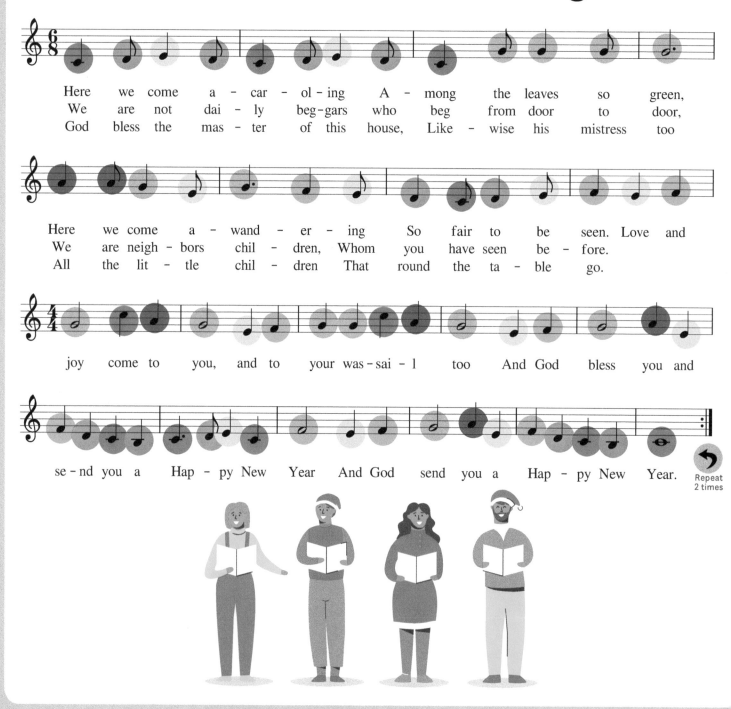

Here we come a - car - ol - ing A - mong the leaves so green,
We are not dai - ly beg-gars who beg from door to door,
God bless the mas - ter of this house, Like - wise his mistress too

Here we come a - wand - er - ing So fair to be seen. Love and
We are neigh - bors chil - dren, Whom you have seen be - fore.
All the lit - tle chil - dren That round the ta - ble go.

joy come to you, and to your was - sai - l too And God bless you and

se - nd you a Hap - py New Year And God send you a Hap - py New Year.

Repeat
2 times

We Wish You a Merry Christmas

Deck the Halls

Deck   the halls with   boughs of hol – ly   Fa – la – la – la – la,   la – la – la – la
See   the blaz – ing   Yule be – fore us
Fast   a – way the   old year pass – es

Tis   the sea – son   to be jol – ly   Fa – la – la – la – la,   la – la – la – la
Strike   the harp and   join the chor – us
Hail   the new, ye   lads and lass – es

Don   we now our   gay ap – par – el   Fa – la – la,   la – la – la,   la – la – la.
Fol – low me in   mer – ry meas – ure
Sing   we joy – ous   all to – geth – er

Troll   the an – cient   Yule – tide Ca – rol   Fa – la – la – la – la,   la – la – la – la.
While   I tell of   Yule – tide treas – ure
Heed – less of the   wind and weath – er

Repeat
2 times

We Three Kings of Orient Are

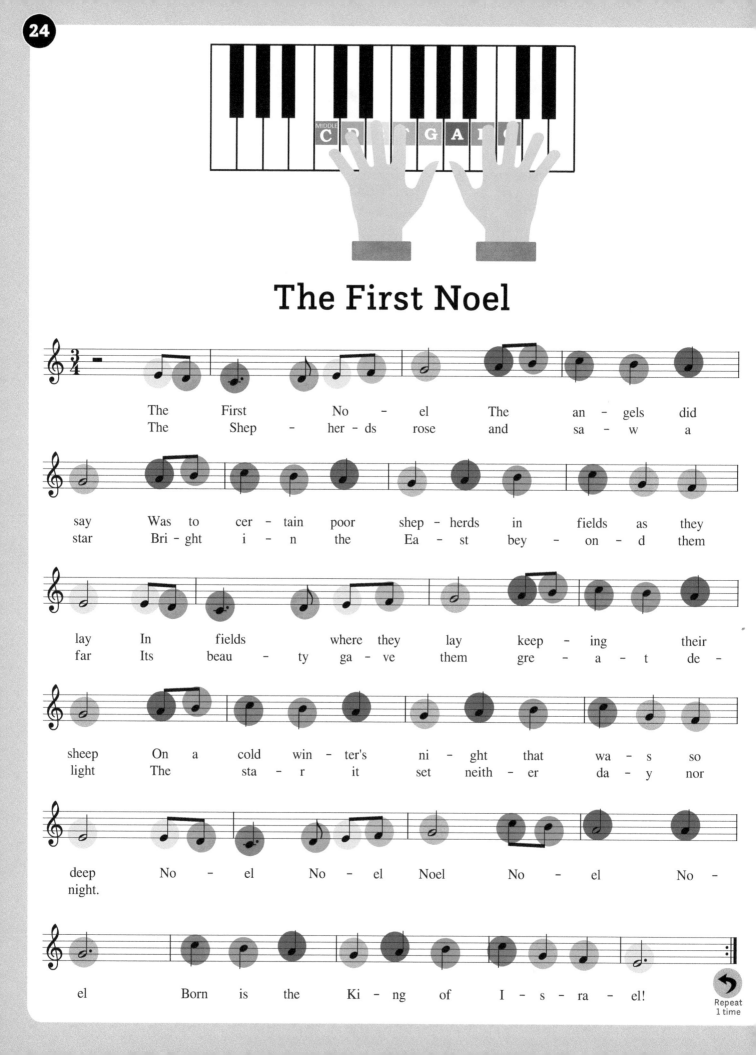

The First Noel

Exercise 5

NEW! You might notice on the songs that follow some strange symbols called **clefs**. Here's what they do:

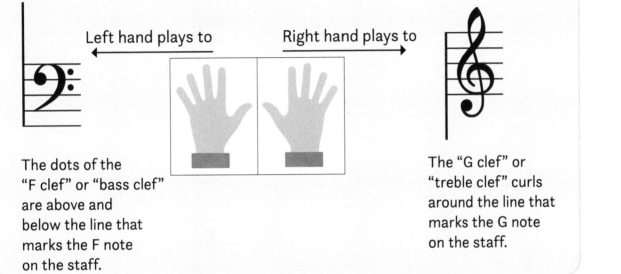

F CLEF

Left hand plays to   Right hand plays to

G CLEF

The dots of the "F clef" or "bass clef" are above and below the line that marks the F note on the staff.

The "G clef" or "treble clef" curls around the line that marks the G note on the staff.

Remember: If you see a symbol that looks like

it is an **Eighth Note Rest** and you will **rest** for **1/2 beat**	it is a **Quarter Note Rest** and you will **rest** for **1 beat**	NEW! it is a **Half Note Rest** and you will **rest** for **2 beats**	you will **rest** for **3 beats**	NEW! it is a **Whole Note Rest** and you will **rest** for **4 beats**

For every song that follows, start with the following **warm-up:**

Clap out the **rhythm** and **sing,**

then practice the **notes** you will play on each hand.

Away in a Manger

A - way in a man - ger no crib for a bed The lit - tle Lord
The cat - tle are low - ing the poor ba - by wakes But lit - tle Lord
Be near me Lord Je - sus I ask thee to stay Close by me for -

Je sus lay down his sweet head The stars in the sk - y look down where he
Je sus no cry - ing he makes I love thee Lord Je - sus look down from the
e ver and love me I pray Bless all the dear chil - dren in Thy ten-der

lay The lit - tle Lord Je - sus a - sleep on the hay.
sky And stay by my si - de til morn ing is nigh.
care And take us to heav - en to live with thee there.

Repeat
2 times

I Saw Three Ships

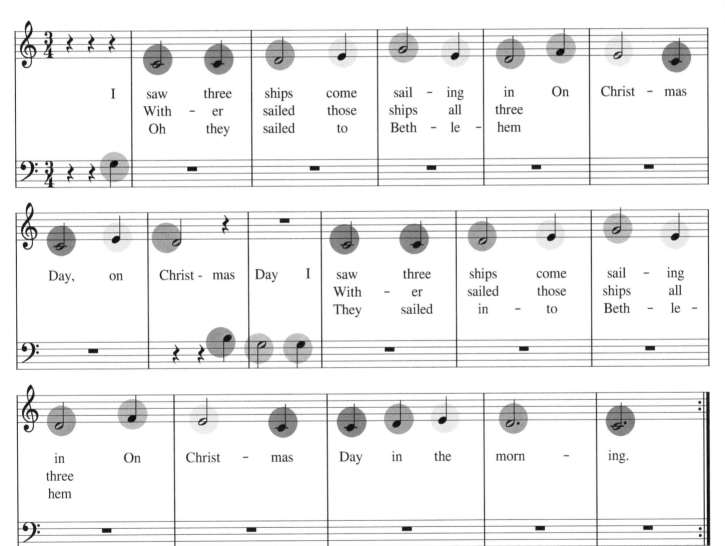

Repeat 2 times

Oh Come All Ye Faithful

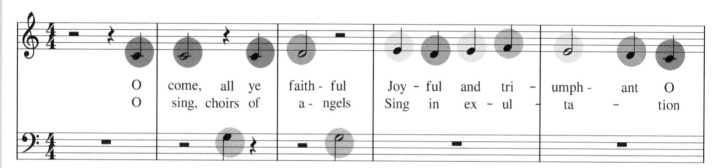

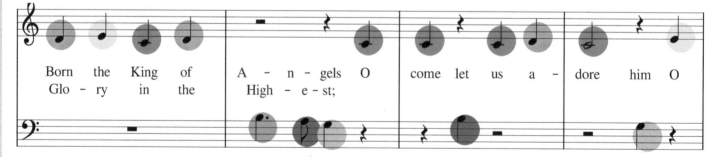

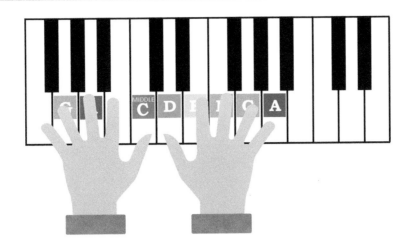

Go Tell It on the Mountain

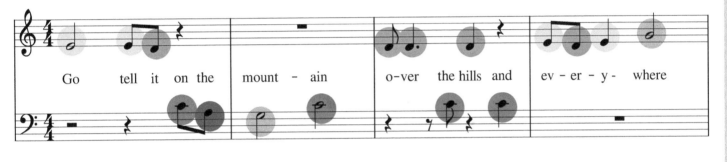

Go tell it on the | mount - ain | o-ver the hills and | ev - er - y- where

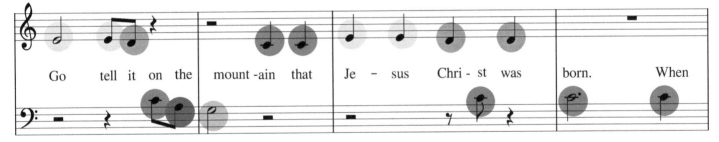

Go tell it on the | mount -ain that | Je — sus Chri - st was | born. When

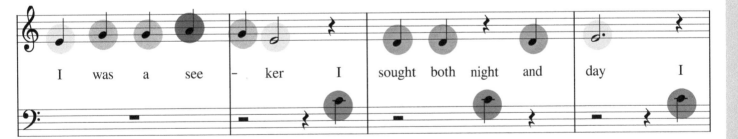

I was a see | - ker I | sought both night and | day I

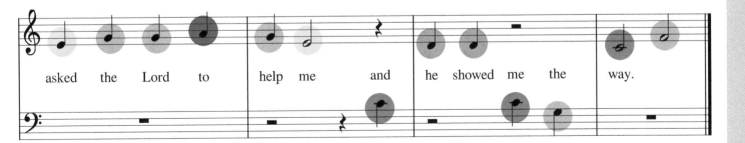

asked the Lord to | help me and | he showed me the | way.

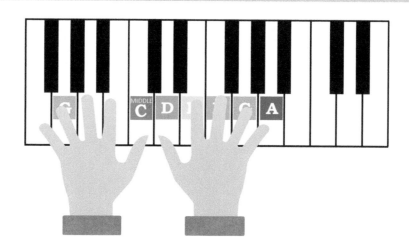

Angels We Have Heard on High

An - gels we have heard on high Sweet - ly sing - ing o'er the plains
Shep - herds why this jub - i - lee? Why your joy - ous strains pro - long?
Come to Beth - le - hem and see Him whose birth the an - gels sing,

And the mount - ains in re - ply Ec - ho - ing their joy - ous strains
What the glad - some ti - dings be Which in - spire your heaven - ly song?
Come a - dore on bend - ed knee, Christ the Lord, the new - born King.

Glo ri - a, in ex - cel - sis De - o

Glo ri - a, in ex - cel - sis De - o.

Repeat
2 times

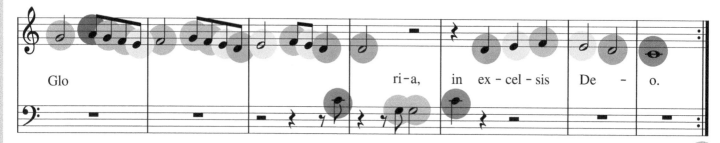

Good King Wenceslas

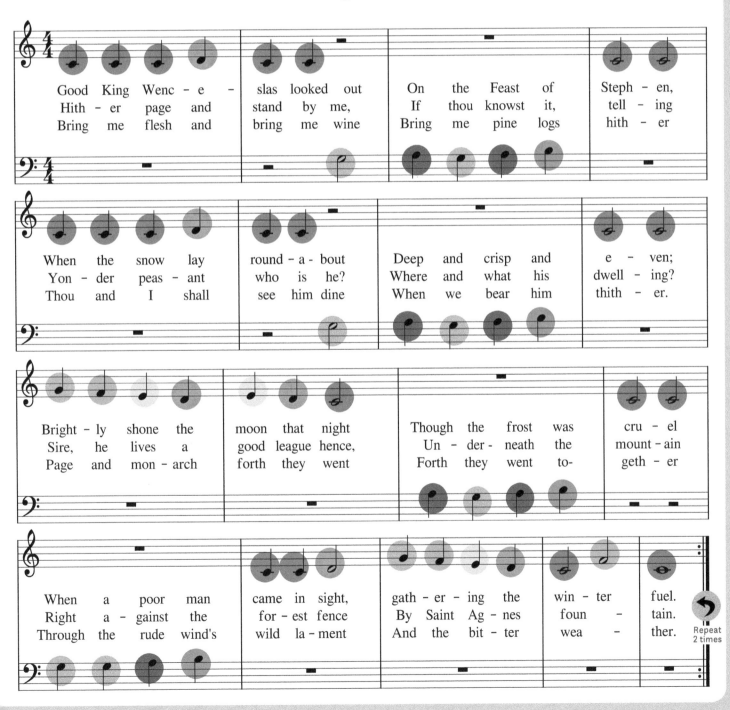

Quiz Time!

Don't worry, you've got this!

Name the **notes** below.

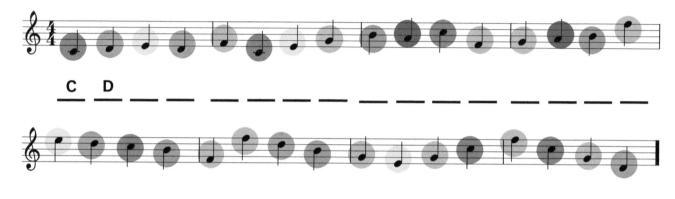

C   D   _   _   _   _   _   _   _   _   _   _   _   _   _   _   _

_   _   _   _   _   _   _   _   _   _   _   _   _   _   _   _   _

How many **beats** does each play for?

1   1   _   _   _   _   _   _   _   _

_   _   _   _   _   _   _   _   _   _   _   _

Complete the sentence:

"If it's in a space, it's part of _____"

"Every good boy _____ _____"

Exercise 6

Play with the correct finger:
Sometimes you will need to move your hand to reach the keys. We number the fingers to show you how to play.

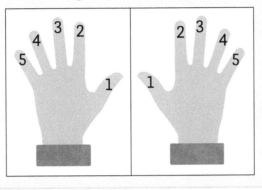

Sharps  **and Flats** ♭

Have you noticed that we're only playing on the white keys? Well, the black keys can also be played. They are called **sharps** and **flats**.

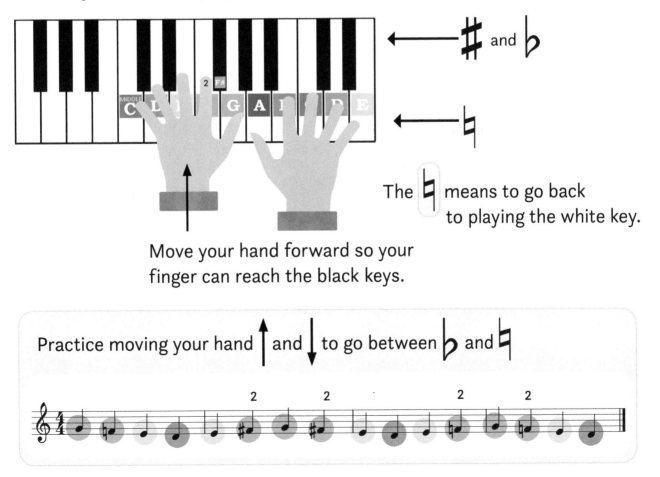

♯ and ♭

♮

The ♮ means to go back to playing the white key.

Move your hand forward so your finger can reach the black keys.

Practice moving your hand ↑ and ↓ to go between ♭ and ♮

O Holy Night

O ho-ly night the stars are bright-ly shin - ing It is the night of our dear Savi-or's

birth Long lay the world in sin and err - or pin - ing Till He a - ppeared and the

soul felt its worth A thrill of hope the wea - ry world re - joice - s For yon-der

breaks a new glor-i - ous morn Fall on your knees O hear the an-gels'

voices O night div - ine O night when Christ was born O

night O night div - ine when Christ was born.

When you see this symbol

Hold for   1,   2,   3,   4,   5

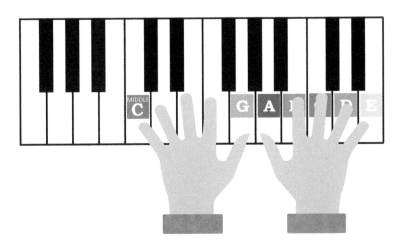

From Starry Skies Thou Comest

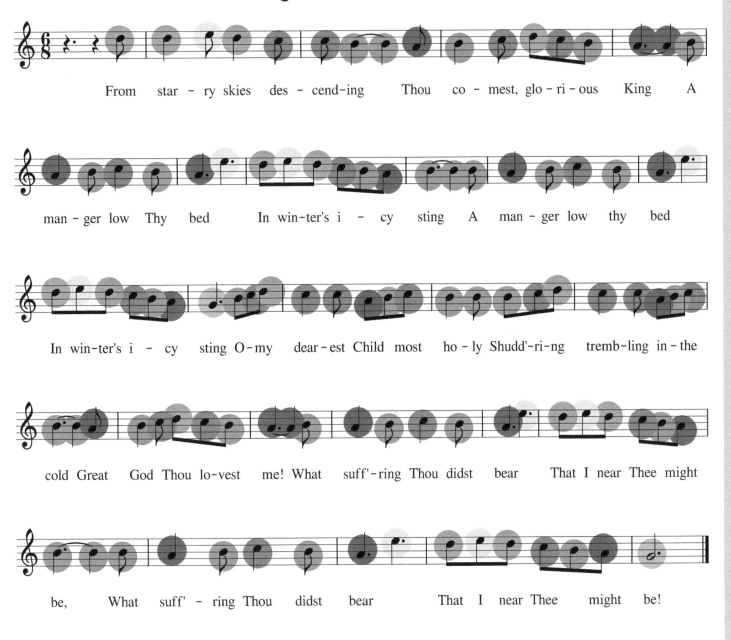

From star - ry skies des - cend-ing Thou co - mest, glo - ri - ous King A

man - ger low Thy bed In win-ter's i - cy sting A man - ger low thy bed

In win-ter's i - cy sting O-my dear-est Child most ho - ly Shudd'-ri-ng tremb-ling in-the

cold Great God Thou lo-vest me! What suff'-ring Thou didst bear That I near Thee might

be, What suff' - ring Thou didst bear That I near Thee might be!

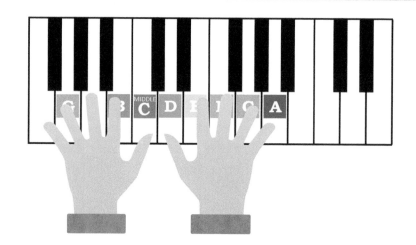

Once in Royal David's City

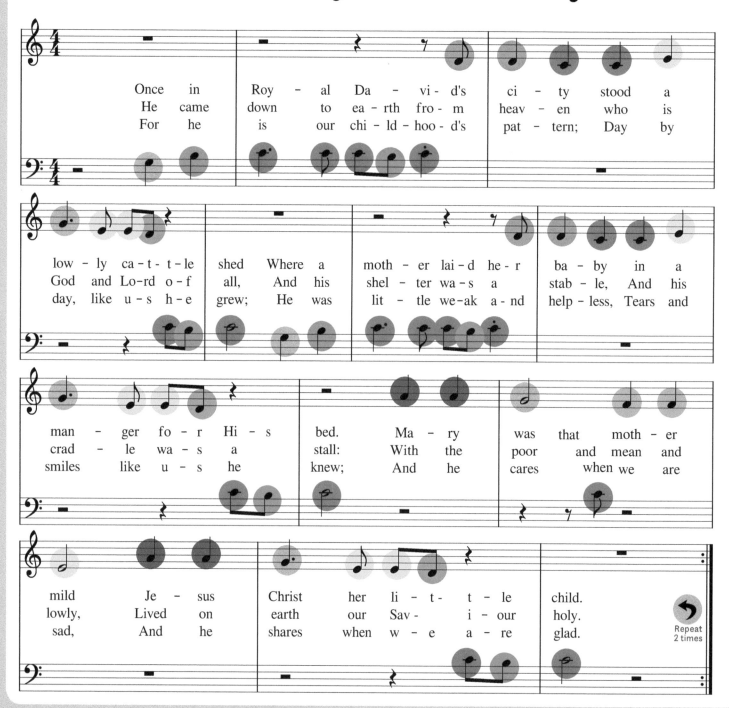

Once in Roy - al Da - vi - d's ci - ty stood a
He came down to ea - rth fro - m heav - en who is
For he is our chi - ld - hoo - d's pat - tern; Day by

low - ly ca - t - t - le shed Where a moth - er lai - d he - r ba - by in a
God and Lo - rd o - f all, And his shel - ter wa - s a stab - le, And his
day, like u - s h - e grew; He was lit - tle we - ak a - nd help - less, Tears and

man - ger fo - r Hi - s bed. Ma - ry was that moth - er
crad - le wa - s a stall: With the poor and mean and
smiles like u - s he knew; And he cares when we are

mild Je - sus Christ her li - t - t - le child.
lowly, Lived on earth our Sav - i - our holy.
sad, And he shares when w - e a - re glad.

Repeat 2 times

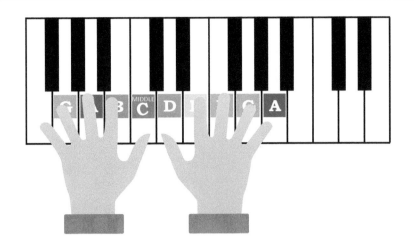

In the Bleak Midwinter

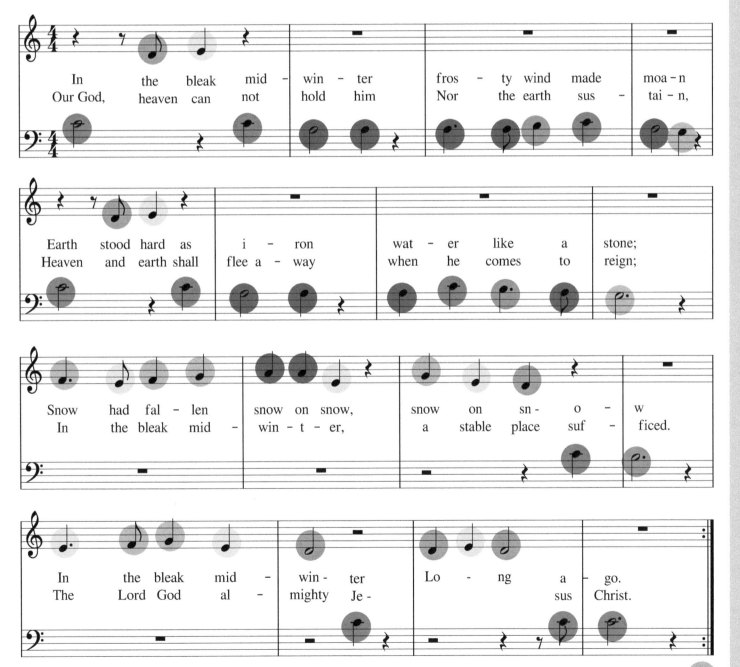

Exercise 7

Remember: The notes are placed on the staff in a specific way.

On the **G clef,** the notes in the **spaces** spell

F A C E

Say it 5 times: *"If it's in a space, it's part of FACE."*

On the **G clef,** the notes in the **lines**

E G B D F

can be remembered in a sentence:

"Every Good Boy Deserves Fudge."

Say it 5 times: *"Every Good Boy Deserves Fudge."*

NEW! On the **F clef,** the notes in the **spaces**

A C E G

can be remembered in a sentence:

"All Cows Eat Grass."

Say it 5 times: *"All Cows Eat Grass."*

NEW! On the **F clef,** the notes in the **lines**

G B D F A

can be remembered in a sentence:

"Good Bikes Don't Fall Apart."

Say it 5 times: *"Good Bikes Don't Fall Apart."*

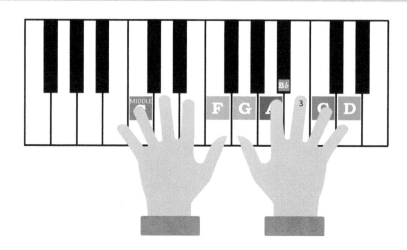

Up on the Housetop

Up   on   the house – top   Rein – deer pause,   Out   jumps good   old   San – ta   Claus
First comes the stock – ing   of   little Nell,   Oh,   dear San – ta   fill   it   well!
Look   in   the stock – ing   of   little Bill,   Oh,   just   see   what   glori – ous fill!

Down through the chim – ney with   lots   of   toys   All   for   the lit – tle ones   Christ – mas joys
Give   her   a   dol – ly that   laughs and cries;   One   that will o – pen and   shut   her   eyes.
Here   is   a   ham – mer and   lots   of tacks   A   whistle and ball and a   whip that cracks!

Ho,   ho,   ho!   Who   would – n't   go   Ho,   ho,   ho!   Who   would – n't   go – o

Up   on   the house – top   Click, click, click   Down   through the chim – ney with   good Saint Nick.

Repeat
2 times

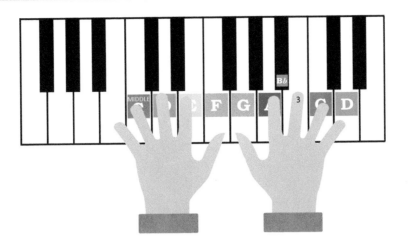

Hark! The Herald Angels Sing

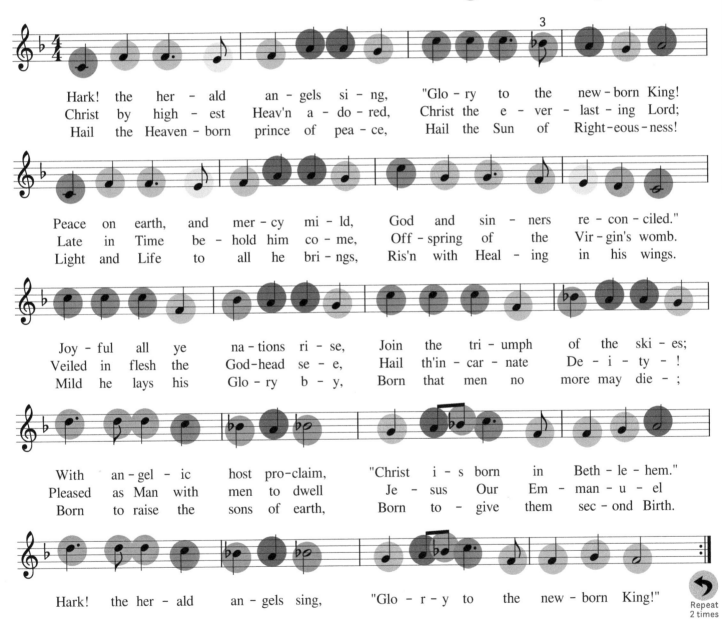

Hark!   the   her - ald   an - gels   si - ng,   "Glo - ry   to   the   new - born King!
Christ   by   high - est   Heav'n a - do - red,   Christ the   e - ver - last - ing Lord;
Hail   the Heaven - born   prince of pea - ce,   Hail the Sun   of   Right-eous - ness!

Peace   on   earth,   and   mer - cy   mi - ld,   God   and   sin - ners   re - con - ciled."
Late   in   Time   be - hold him   co - me,   Off - spring   of   the   Vir - gin's womb.
Light   and   Life   to   all   he   bri - ngs,   Ris'n   with   Heal - ing   in   his   wings.

Joy - ful   all   ye   na - tions   ri - se,   Join   the   tri - umph   of   the   ski - es;
Veiled   in   flesh   the   God-head   se - e,   Hail   th'in - car - nate   De - i - ty - !
Mild   he   lays   his   Glo - ry   b - y,   Born   that   men   no   more may   die - ;

With   an - gel - ic   host pro-claim,   "Christ   i - s   born   in   Beth - le - hem."
Pleased   as Man   with   men   to dwell   Je - sus   Our   Em - man - u - el
Born   to raise   the   sons   of earth,   Born   to - give   them   sec - ond Birth.

Hark!   the   her - ald   an - gels sing,   "Glo - r - y   to   the   new - born   King!"

Repeat
2 times

The 12 Days of Christmas

On the | first day of Christ-mas my | true love gave to me, a | part-ri-dge in a pear | tree. On the

sec-ond day of Christ-mas my | true love gave to me, | Two tur-tle doves and a | par-tri-dge in a pear

tree. On the | third day of Christ-mas my | true love gave to me, | Three fre-nch hens, | Two tur-tle doves and a

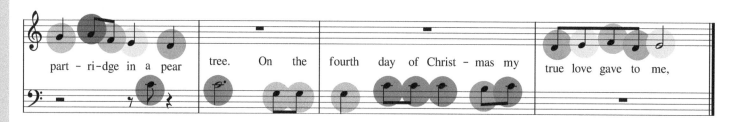

part-ri-dge in a pear | tree. On the | fourth day of Christ-mas my | true love gave to me,

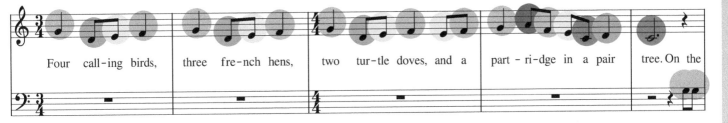

Four call-ing birds, three fre-nch hens, two tur-tle doves, and a part - ri-dge in a pair tree. On the

fifth day of Christ-mas my true love gave to me, Five gold-en rings Fo - ur call-ing birds,

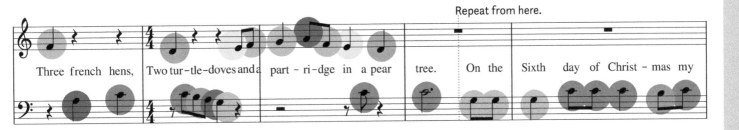

Repeat from here.

Three french hens, Two tur-tle-doves and a part - ri-dge in a pear tree. On the Sixth day of Christ - mas my

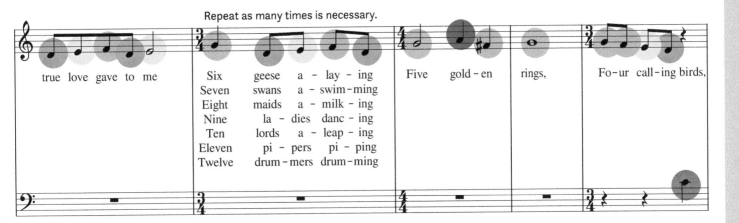

Repeat as many times is necessary.

true love gave to me

Six	geese	a - lay - ing
Seven	swans	a - swim-ming
Eight	maids	a - milk - ing
Nine	la - dies	danc - ing
Ten	lords	a - leap - ing
Eleven	pi - pers	pi - ping
Twelve	drum-mers	drum-ming

Five gold-en rings, Fo-ur call-ing birds,

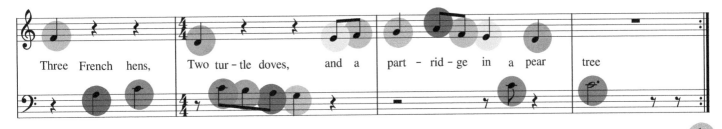

Three French hens, Two tur - tle doves, and a part - rid-ge in a pear tree

Repeat
6 times

Exercise 8

Naming the hand positions: Hand position is named for the key the thumb is on.

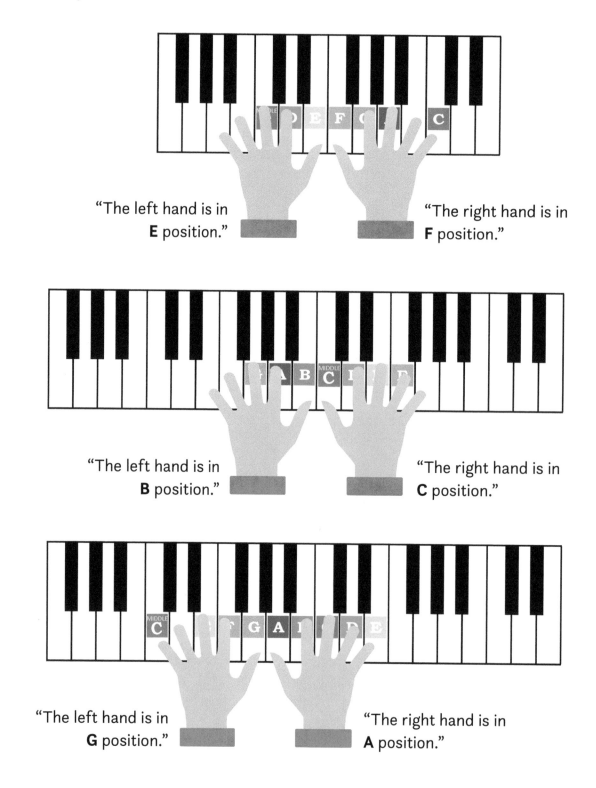

"The left hand is in
E position."

"The right hand is in
F position."

"The left hand is in
B position."

"The right hand is in
C position."

"The left hand is in
G position."

"The right hand is in
A position."

Quiz Time!

Don't worry, you've got this!
Name the **hand positions** on the keyboards below.

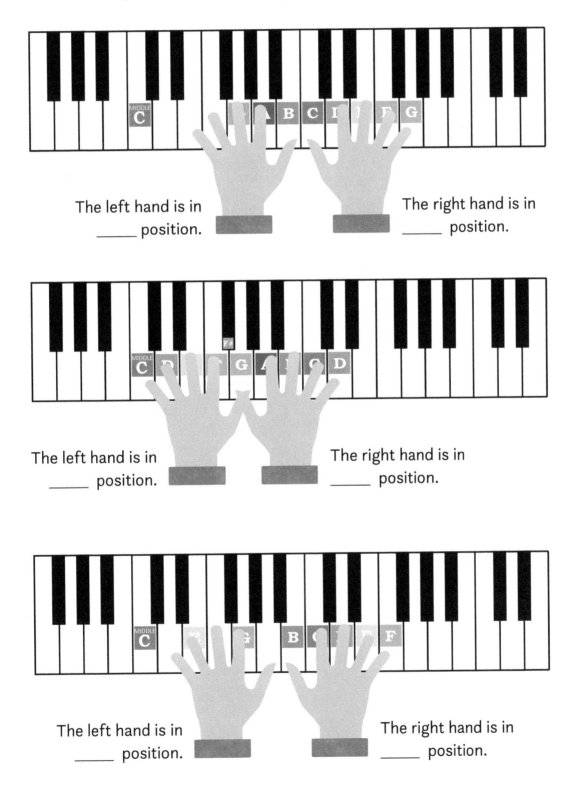

The left hand is in
_____ position.

The right hand is in
_____ position.

The left hand is in
_____ position.

The right hand is in
_____ position.

The left hand is in
_____ position.

The right hand is in
_____ position.

Gloucestershire Wassail

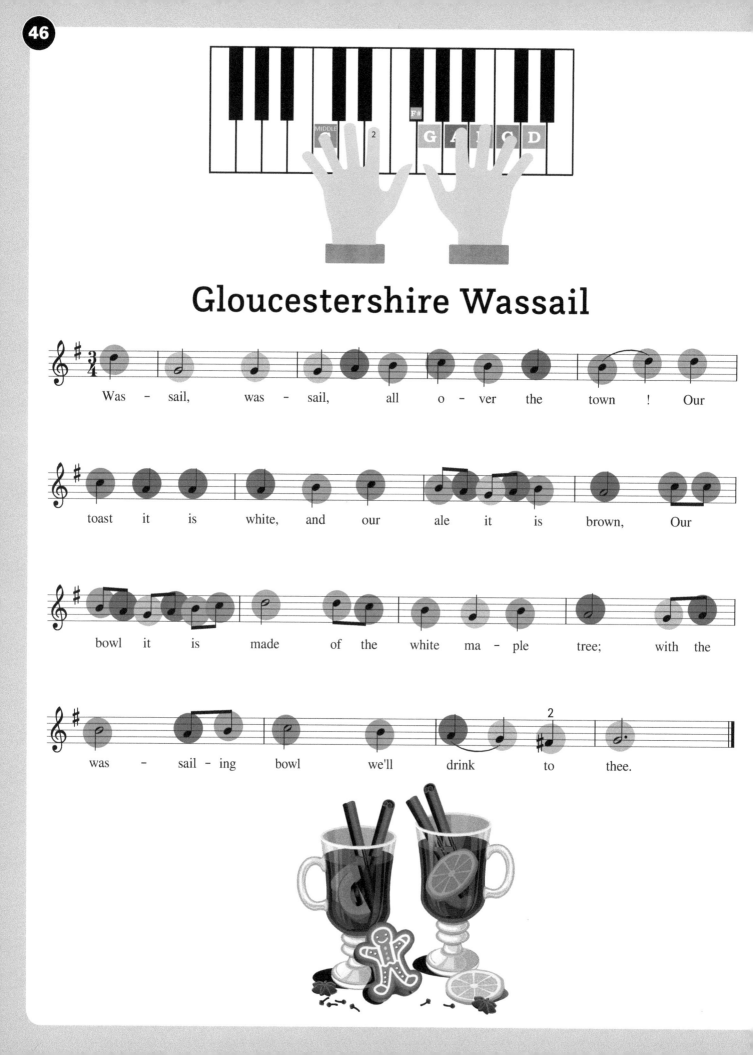

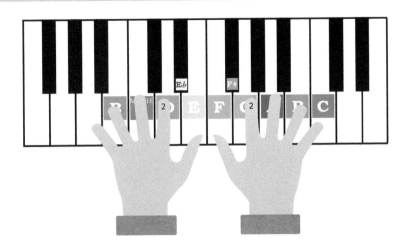

I Heard the Bells on Christmas Day

I	heard	the	bells	on	Christ	–	mas	day	Their
The	bells	are	ring	– ing	Peace		on	earth	Like
And	in	des – pair		I	bowed		my	head	There
Then	rang	the	bells	more	loud		and	deep	God

old	fa	– mil	– iar	car	– ols	play	And	mild	and	sweet	their
a choir	they're	sing	– ing	Peace	on	earth	In	my	heart	I	hear
is	no	peace	on	earth	I	said	For	hate	is	strong	and
is	not	dead,	nor	does	he	sleep	The	wrong	shall	fail,	the

songs	re – peat	Of	peace	on	earth	good	– will	to	men.
hear	them								
mocks	the song								
right	pre – vail								

Repeat 3 times

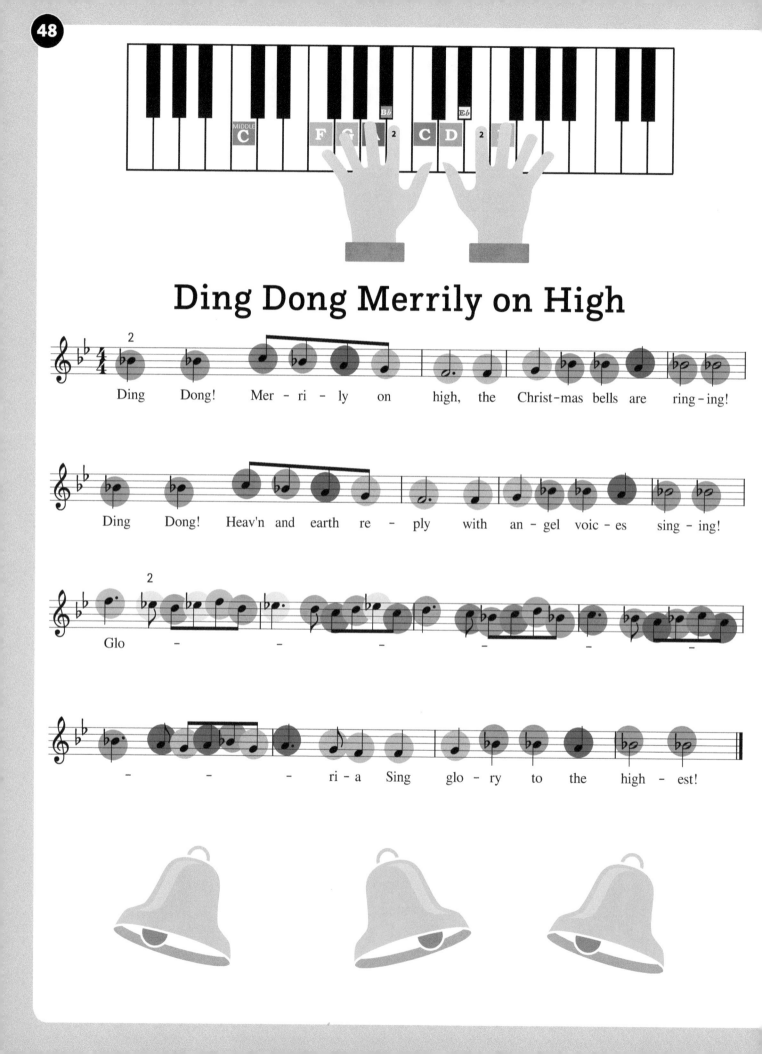

Ding Dong Merrily on High

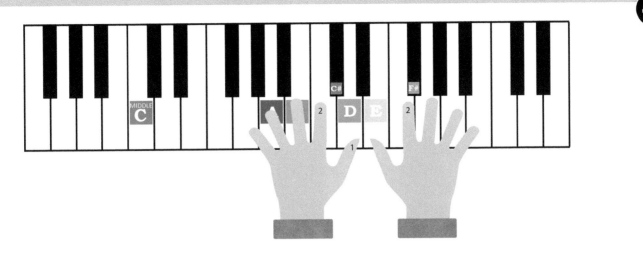

Hallelujah Chorus (Handel's *Messiah*)

Hal – le - lu - jah, Hal - le - lu - jah, Hal - le - lu - jah, Hal-le-lu-jah, Hal - le - lu - jah,

Hal – le - lu - jah, Hal – le - lu - jah, Hal - le - lu - jah, Hal-le-lu-jah, Hal - le - lu - jah:

for the Lord Godom-ni - po-tent reign - eth, Hal-le - lu-jah, Halle-lu-jah, Halle - lu-jah, Hal-le-lu-jah,

It Came Upon a Midnight Clear

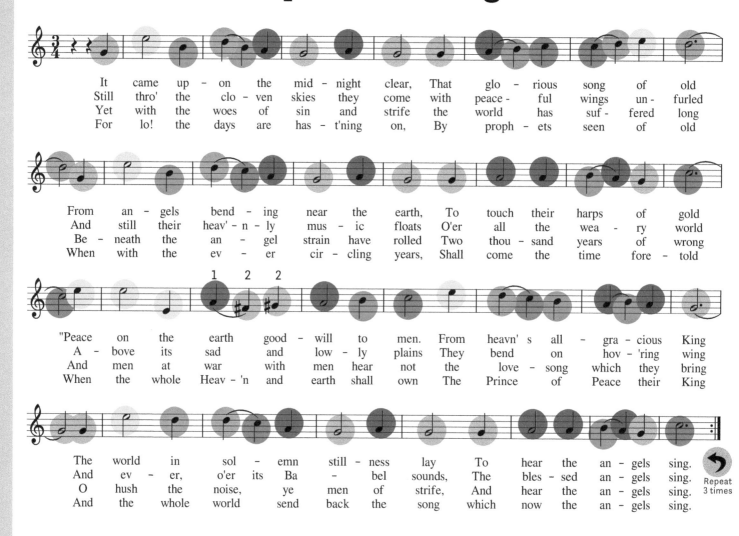

It came up – on the mid – night clear, That glo – rious song of old
Still thro' the clo – ven skies they come with peace – ful wings un – furled
Yet with the woes of sin and strife the world has suf – fered long
For lo! the days are has – t'ning on, By proph – ets seen of old

From an – gels bend – ing near the earth, To touch their harps of gold
And still their heav' – n – ly mus – ic floats O'er all the wea – ry world
Be – neath the an – gel strain have rolled Two thou – sand years of wrong
When with the ev – er cir – cling years, Shall come the time fore – told

"Peace on the earth good – will to men. From heavn's all – gra – cious King
A – bove its earth sad and low – ly plains They bend on hov – 'ring wing
And men at war with men hear not the love – song which they bring
When the whole Heav – 'n and earth shall own The Prince of Peace their King

The world in sol – emn still – ness lay To hear the an – gels sing.
And ev – er, o'er its Ba – bel sounds, The bles – sed an – gels sing.
O hush the noise, ye men of strife, And hear the an – gels sing.
And the whole world send back the song which now the an – gels sing.

Repeat 3 times

What Child is This?

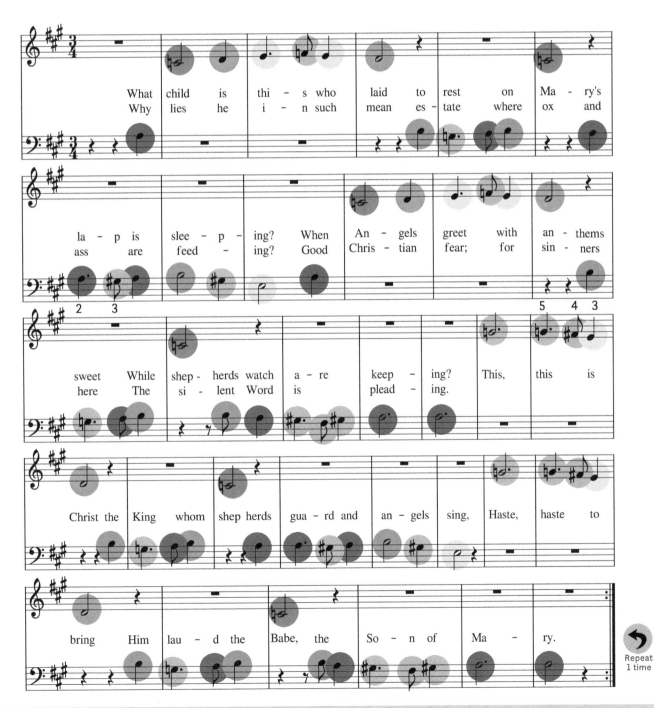

Repeat
1 time

Exercise 9

NEW! Changing the hand positions: **Jumping**
Sometimes if one hand is playing and the other resting, the resting
hand will **jump** over the other to help play the notes.

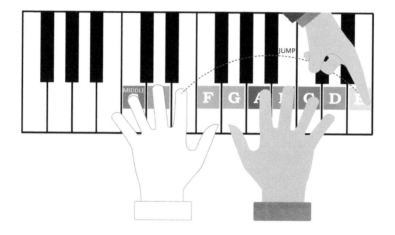

Practice the following exercise, with the left hand jumping back
and forth over the right to play the notes for "Oh Little Town
of Bethlehem" on page 53.

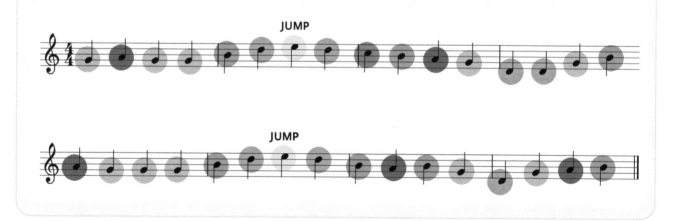

1 Practice the jumped musical phrase **5 times**.

2 Pay attention to the position of your thumb,
so you can return to the original hand position easily.

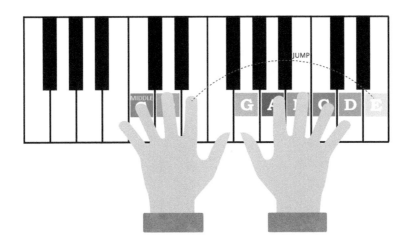

Oh Little Town of Bethlehem

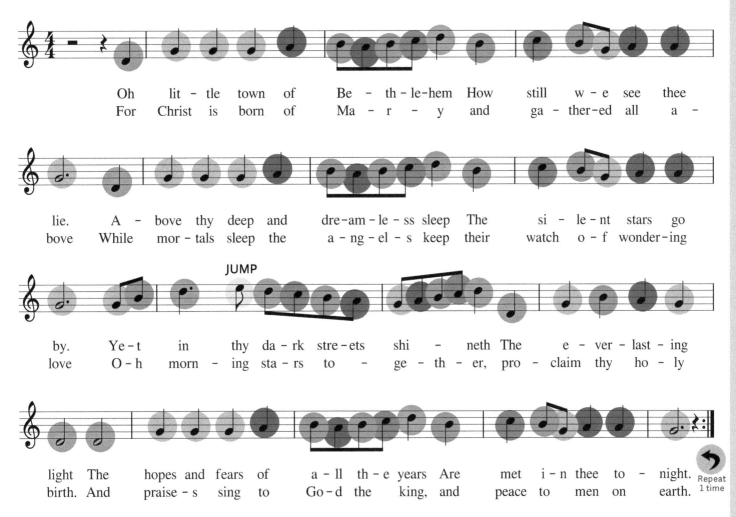

Oh   lit – tle   town   of   Be – th–le–hem How   still   w – e   see   thee
For   Christ   is   born   of   Ma – r – y   and   ga – ther–ed all   a –

lie.   A – bove thy   deep   and   dre–am–le – ss sleep The   si – le – nt stars   go
bove While mor – tals sleep   the   a – ng–el – s keep their   watch o – f wonder–ing

by.   Ye – t   in   thy   da – rk stre–ets   shi –   neth The   e – ver – last – ing
love   O – h   morn – ing sta – rs to –   ge – th – er, pro – claim thy   ho – ly

light   The   hopes and fears   of   a – ll th – e years   Are   met   i – n thee to – night.
birth. And   praise – s sing   to   Go – d   the   king, and   peace   to   men   on   earth.

Repeat
1 time

Exercise 10

More jumping: Practice playing the notes for "Auld Lang Syne" on page 55.

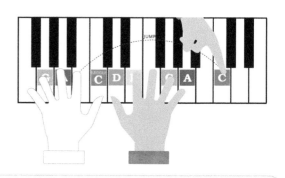

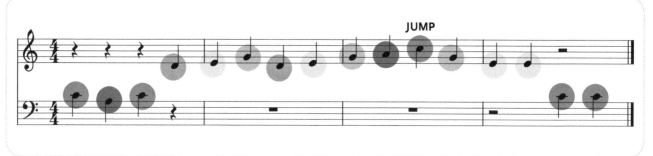

Practice playing the notes for "O Christmas Tree" on page 56.

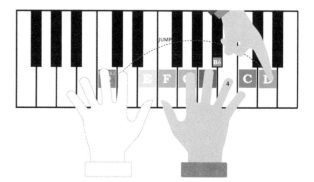

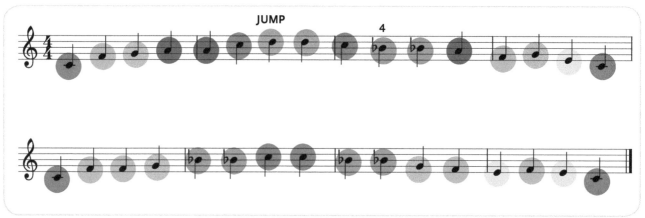

1 Practice the jumped musical phrase **5 times**.

2 Pay attention to the position of your thumb, so you can return to the original hand position easily.

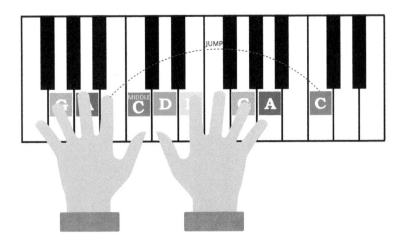

Auld Lang Syne

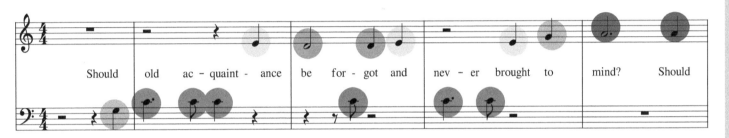

Should old ac - quaint - ance be for - got and nev - er brought to mind? Should

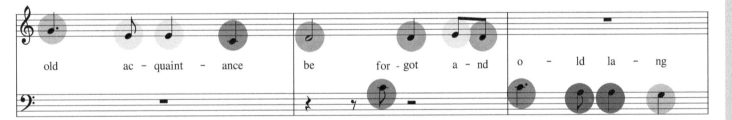

old ac - quaint - ance be for - got a - nd o - ld la - ng

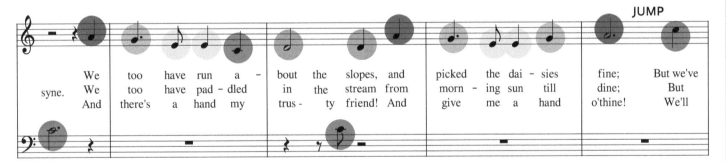

JUMP

syne. We too have run a - bout the slopes, and picked the dai - sies fine; But we've

We too have pad - dled in the stream from morn - ing sun till dine; But

And there's a hand my trus - ty friend! And give me a hand o'thine! We'll

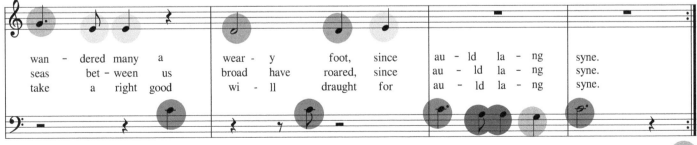

wan - dered many a wear - y foot, since au - ld la - ng syne.

seas bet - ween us broad have roared, since au - ld la - ng syne.

take a right good wi - ll draught for au - ld la - ng syne.

Repeat
2 times

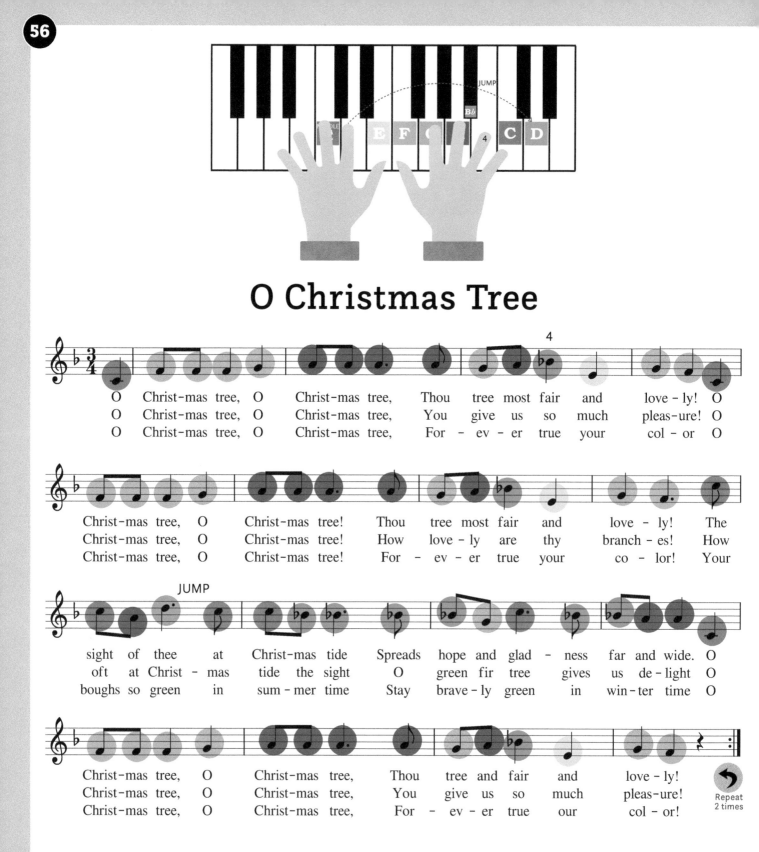

O Christmas Tree

Exercise 11

NEW! Changing the hand positions: **Sliding**
Sometimes you will **slide** your hands up or down the keyboard to play the notes.

In the example below, hands move together so both thumbs go down **one key**: left thumb Ⓐ to Ⓖ, right thumb Ⓑ to Ⓐ. The other fingers follow.

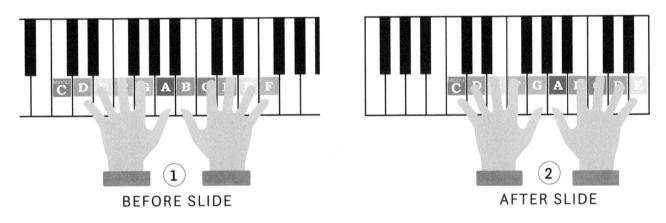

BEFORE SLIDE   AFTER SLIDE

Practice playing the notes for "Silent Night" on page 58.

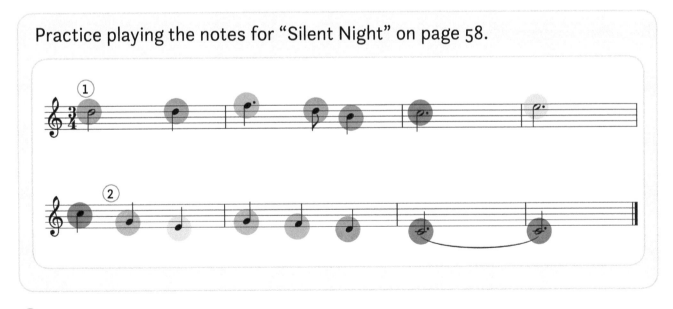

❶ Move your hands together.

❷ Pay attention to the position of your thumbs, and keep them on keys next to each other when possible.

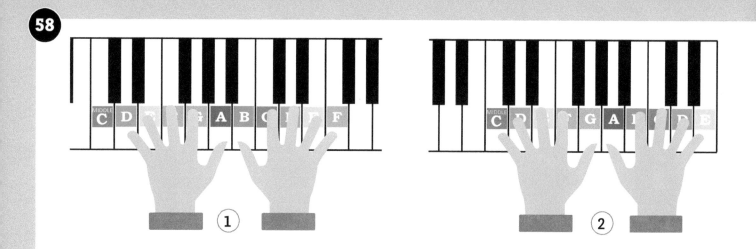

Silent Night

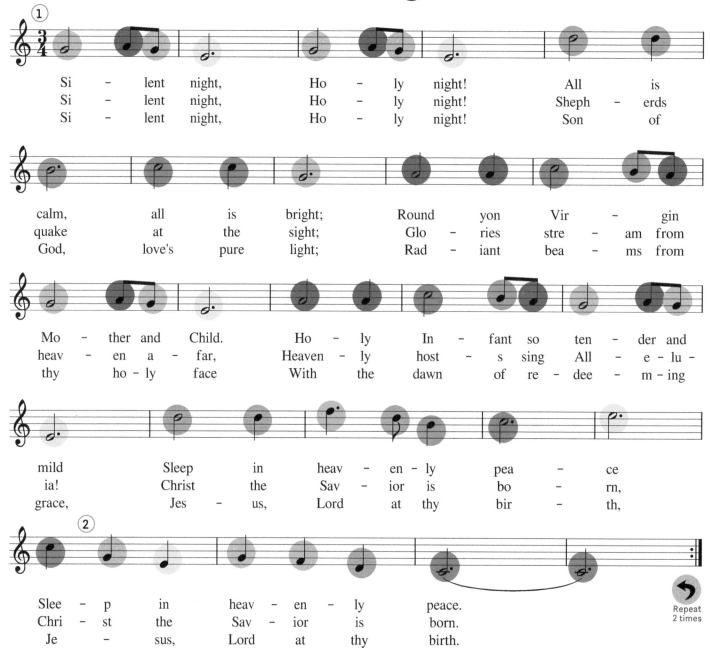

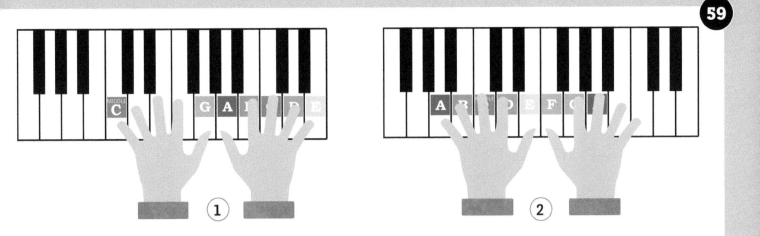

God Rest Ye Merry Gentlemen

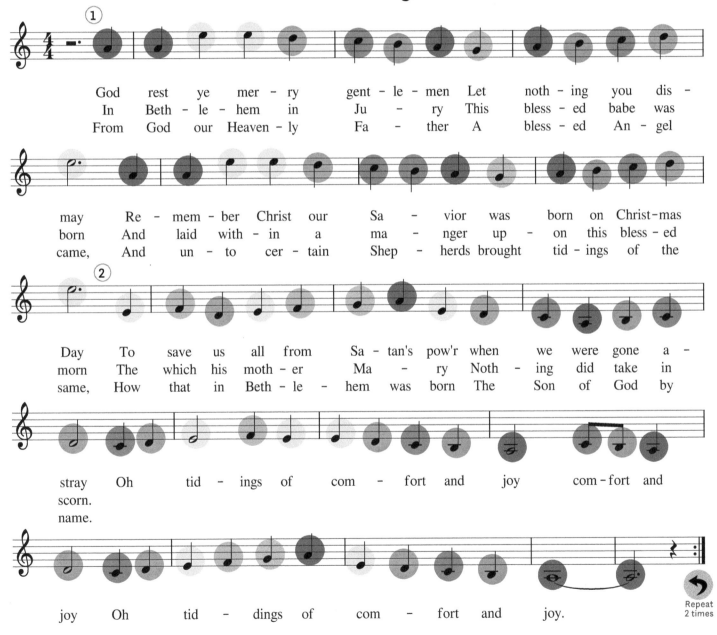

God rest ye mer – ry gent – le – men Let noth – ing you dis –
In Beth – le – hem in Ju – ry This bless – ed babe was
From God our Heaven – ly Fa – ther A bless – ed An – gel

may Re – mem – ber Christ our Sa – vior was born on Christ-mas
born And laid with – in a ma – nger up – on this bless – ed
came, And un – to cer – tain Shep – herds brought tid – ings of the

Day To save us all from Sa – tan's pow'r when we were gone a –
morn The which his moth – er Ma – ry Noth – ing did take in
same, How that in Beth – le – hem was born The Son of God by

stray Oh tid – ings of com – fort and joy com – fort and
scorn.
name.

joy Oh tid – dings of com – fort and joy.

Repeat
2 times

Quiz Time!

Don't worry, you've got this!

Name the **notes** below.

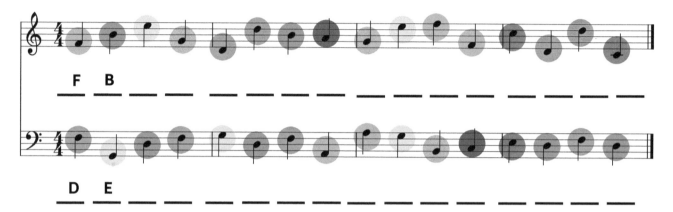

F   B _____ _____ _____ _____ _____ _____ _____

D   E _____ _____ _____ _____ _____ _____ _____

Complete the sentence:

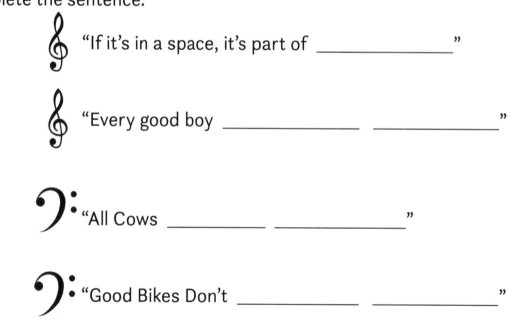

𝄞 "If it's in a space, it's part of _____"

𝄞 "Every good boy _____ _____"

𝄢 "All Cows _____ _____"

𝄢 "Good Bikes Don't _____ _____"

Exercise 12

NEW! Changing the hand positions: **Stretching**
Sometimes you won't need to fully slide your hand to reach a key; instead just **stretch** the hand wide for the pinky to reach.

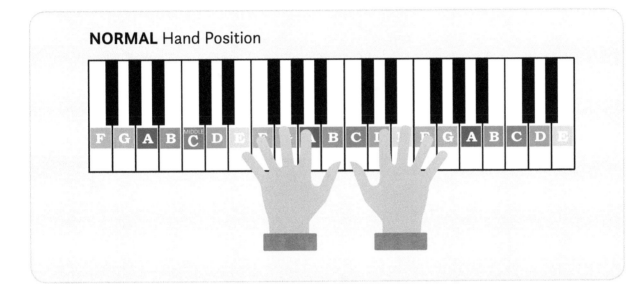

NORMAL Hand Position

Stretch your hand to reach more keys

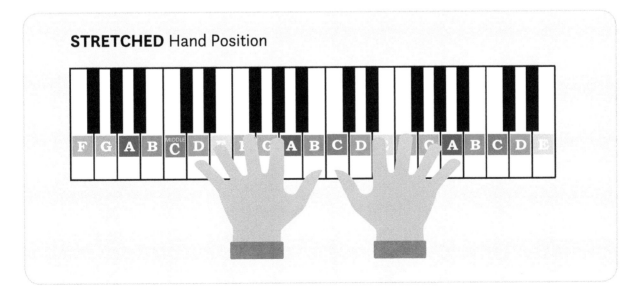

STRETCHED Hand Position

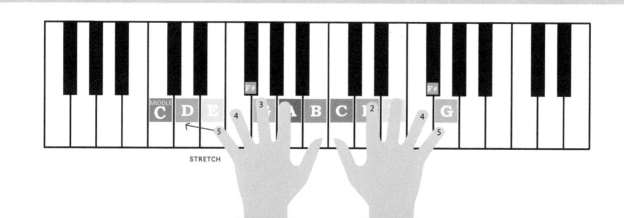

Jesu, Joy of Man's Desiring

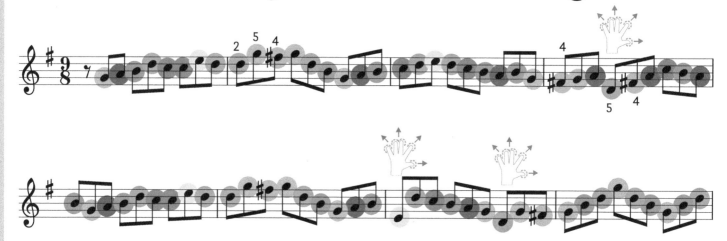

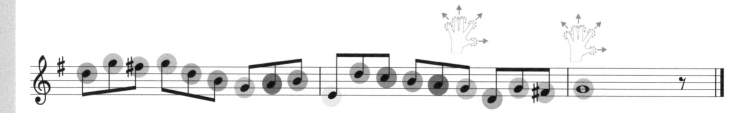

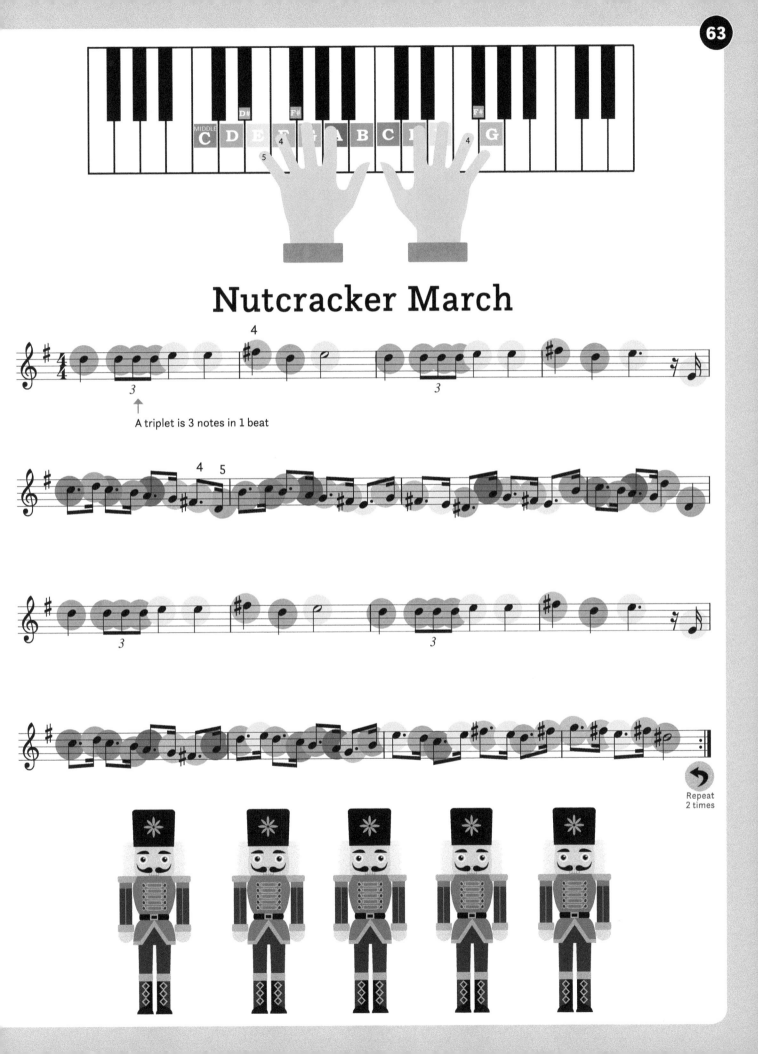

Nutcracker March

A triplet is 3 notes in 1 beat

Repeat
2 times

Cut the labels below and attach them to your piano keys as shown on page 8.

Standard size piano key labels

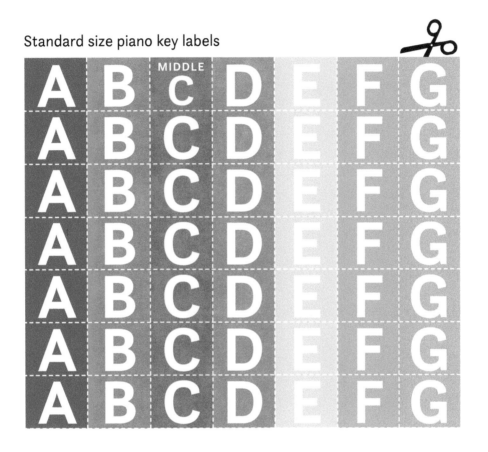

Mini key labels

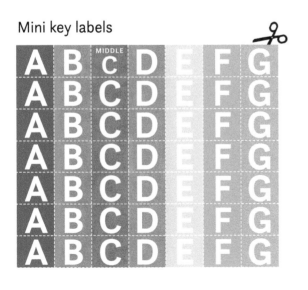

Mid-size piano key labels

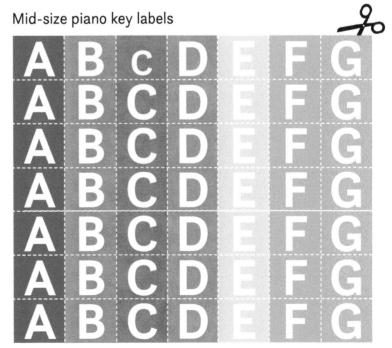

Cut the labels below and attach them to your piano keys as shown on page 8.

Standard size piano key labels

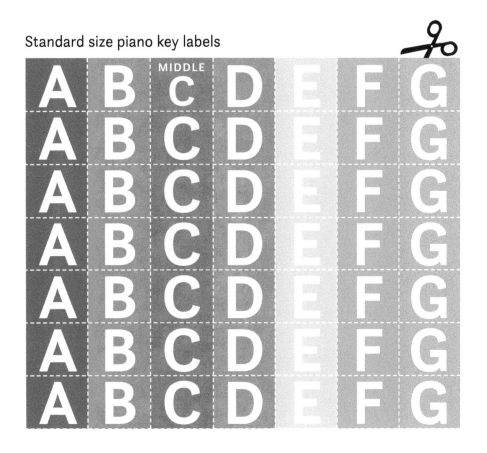

Mini key labels

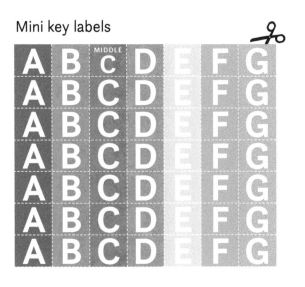

Mid-size piano key labels

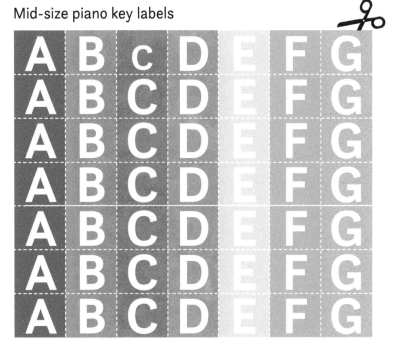

Congratulations!

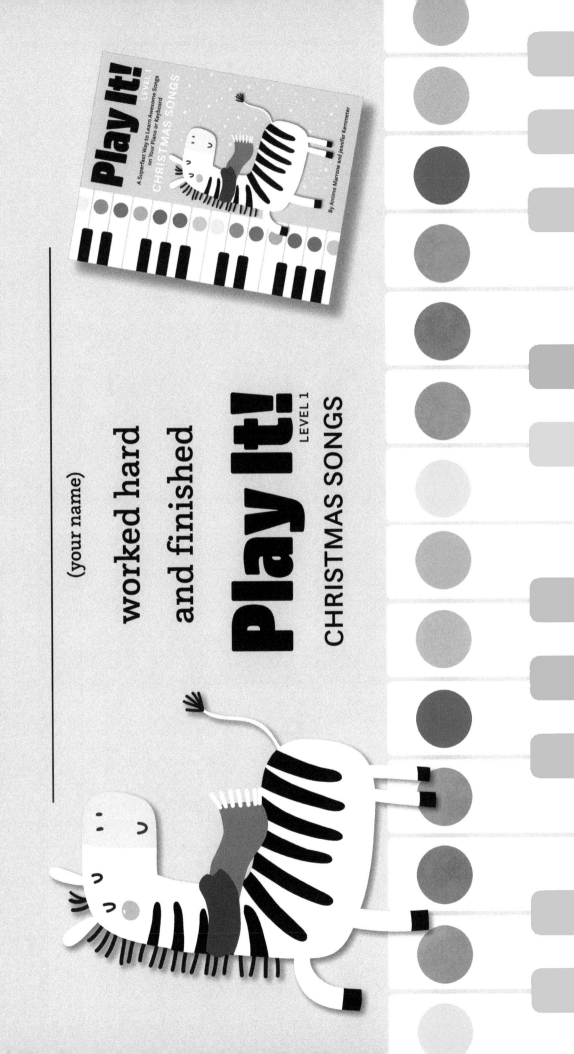

(your name)

worked hard
and finished

Play It!
LEVEL 1
CHRISTMAS SONGS

Make sure your

Play It!

library is complete